Esa-Pekka Salonen

CONCERT ÉTUDE

for solo horn in F

CHESTER MUSIC

Exclusive distributors:
Hal Leonard
7777 West Bluemound Road, Milwaukee, WI 53213
Email: info@halleonard.com

Hal Leonard Europe Limited
42 Wigmore Street Marylebone, London, WIU 2 RY
Email: info@halleonardeurope.com

Hal Leonard Australia Pty. Ltd.
4 Lentara Court Cheltenham, Victoria, 9132 Australia
Email: info@halleonard.com.au

This work was commissioned by the Lieksa Brass Week, Finland, for the Holger Fransman Memorial Competition, 2000.

Duration: c. 6 minutes

Score on sale: Order No. CH61768

ISBN 0-7119-9894-9

Notation

⌃	Short fermata	↓	¼ tone flat
⌐·	Long fermata	⟱	¾ tone flat
⊕	Half stopped	‡	¼ tone sharp

COMPOSER'S NOTE

I will never forget my first French horn lesson with Holger Fransman. For an eleven-year-old boy the great Finnish musician and teacher was an awesome sight: an impressive moustache and fiery eyes. He used to call me Mr Salonen despite my age, and only after I could play to the top C with some accuracy did he suggest we start addressing each other by first names.

I spent hours every day with the *Waldhornschule* by Oscar Franz, starting with triads for the natural horn, and gradually moving on to chromatic scales using the valves. The very last section of the *Waldhornschule* contained hair-raisingly difficult "real" compositions called "Konzert-Etüden". The title really whetted my appetite, and I kept practising these little pieces feverishly, hoping that one day I would be a great horn player, worthy of my teacher.

Life took a different turn later, and I became a conductor and a composer instead. I never lost contact with Holger, however, and he never missed my concerts in Helsinki. There would always be a phone call the morning after, and Holger's creaky voice would deliver an often quite harsh view of what he had heard. Always to the point, I now have to admit.

I saw him for the last time on his deathbed in a hospital in Helsinki. When I entered the room he was listening to *Ein Heldenleben* on his portable CD-player. His eyes were closed, but he knew I was there. Finally he spoke: "Why, it is the Vienna Philharmonic and yet the timpani are too sharp!" We spoke a bit later about this and that, but these are his last words I can remember.

When I was asked to write a piece for solo horn for the Holger Fransman Memorial Competition, I agreed right away. I decided to write my own *Concert étude* and thus create a little homage to my teacher who, in fact, was like a grandfather to me.

In this piece I treat the horn as a virtuoso instrument, capable of acrobatics as well as idiomatic melodic expression. In a way, I wrote the piece for the great horn player I never became.

E-P.S.

CONCERT ÉTUDE

for Solo Horn in F

Holger Fransman in Memoriam

Esa-Pekka Salonen

CH61768

2

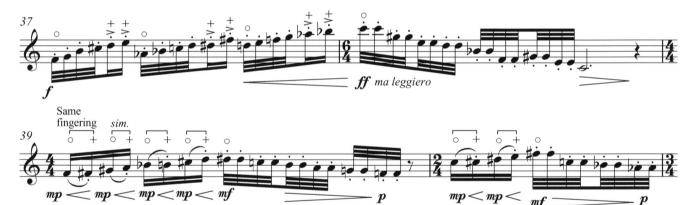

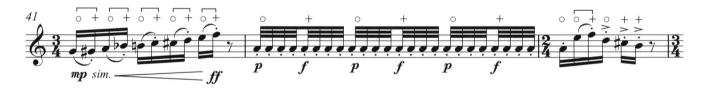

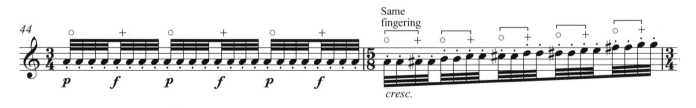